On the Trail

Guyla Nelson

and

Saundra Scovell Lamgo

*Illustrated by David Grassnick
and Hermann C. Grassnick*

American Language Series
A Vowel Digraph Reader

Alpha Omega Publications
Chandler, Arizona

Printed in the United States of America

ISBN 0-86717-992-9

For all boys and girls
who wish to
become readers of
good books —
and especially the
Book of Books, the Bible

Stories

We Will Praise Him

We will give praise to God.

We will thank Him for rain.

We will thank Him for the sun.

We will thank Him for grass and grain.

We will thank Him for Mom and Dad.

We will thank Him for His love.

We will give praise to God.

On the Trail

It is time for a hike. We will take the main trail. There is no rail to aid us as we climb to the top.

I hope it will not rain. If it rains or hails, the trail will be wet. Then there will be lots of mud on the trail.

We do not want to get off the trail and get lost. We hope to climb to the top by dark.

The Breeze

I like the nice feel of the warm breeze. I do not see the breeze, but I feel it on my feet. I feel it on my cheeks. I see it in the green trees. I feel it swish my sleeves. The breeze feels nice.

It is fun to run and skip in the breeze. It fills me with glee. It makes me feel as free as a bird.

Two Flags in the Breeze

Two flags flap in the breeze. The flag on the right pole stands for my land. It waves for the brave and the free. The flag on the left pole stands for my Lord. It waves to tell that He gave His life on the cross for me.

I will not jeer or sneer at these flags. I love them. I love this land. I love God.

The Deer

The deer stands at the edge of the creek. Close by is a clump of tall green trees. He stands quite still. The deer hopes he will not be seen.

He needs to get a drink from the creek. He will peer to the right and to the left. He will peer to the back and to the front.

Then if all seems safe, he will get his drink in the creek as fast as he can.

God helps the deer to be fleet. The deer can run fast. He can speed to the green trees and be safe.

Free Rent!

What a swarm of bees!

These bees have left the old hive.

The queen bee and the bees who work must seek a place to make a fresh hive.

Will the swarm of bees make the hive on the stop sign? Can the bees live so close to the street?

What a place to live! The rent will be free!

A Kind Deed

Lee and I will go to the lake next week. We will stand on the bank of the deep lake and watch for the geese to come.

The geese will swim with much
speed to meet us. As the geese get
close, we will see a nice sheen on the
black necks.

Lee will feed seeds to the geese. I
will feed them cheese.

More geese will fly to meet us. It is a
kind deed for us to feed the geese.

The Snails

I will sail my ship. I will sail it on the lake.

I see snails in the lake. I will aim my ship past the snails. I do not wish to hurt the snails. I just want to watch them.

It is fun to watch a snail walk. It is fun to see a snail get in his shell. I like to see him make a "smoke screen" so that he can hide from a big fish. God made him like this.

Mom's Soap

Mom will make soap. She will make the soap on the stove. I will watch the soap foam in the pan. Mom will use the soap to soak my coat. Mom makes fine soap.

My coat had a bad spot on it. Mom's soap got rid of the bad spot.

Thank Thee, Lord

Thanks for rain
and pain.

Thanks for bees
and cheese.

Thanks for deer
and cheer.

Thanks for goats
and coats.

Thanks that we can
see all God has made for us.

A Bad Goat

The goat feeds by the oak tree. He likes to feed on oats, grass, and trees. The goat likes to roam. At times he roams up the road. Once he ate a coat off the clothes line. This made Cain moan and moan.

Once he ate the beets and corn by the fence. What a bad goat!

When the goat roams, Cain must find him. At times the goat will be close to Cain. At times Cain must use a big stick to make the goat go straight home.

Five Loaves

The lad came up the long road to the hill. He sat on the grass with his lunch. "This high hill will make a nice place to have my lunch," he spoke with glee. "It is fun to sit here and watch the boats on the coast."

Much time went by. The lad did not think of his lunch. A man came and spoke to the lad. He told the lad, "The Lord needs these loaves and fish." He did not have to coax the lad. The lad gave his lunch for the Lord to use.

Jeff's Boat

Jeff has a boat. The boat is green and maize. The boat has a sail.

Jeff floats his boat in the creek. The breeze will make the boat float past the oak tree. The breeze will make the boat float past the toad as it rests on the pad.

Jeff must run on the bank to keep up with his boat.

Strange Fruit

Mom and Dad will cruise in a plane to a warm land. Mom and Dad will bring back fresh fruit.

This fruit will be strange to us. We do not have this kind of fruit at home. We think we will like the taste of this fruit.

We will be glad when Mom and Dad cruise home on the plane.

20

Which Is Which?

Brent and Trent are twins. The twins have on suits that are just the same. I am not sure which lad is Brent. I am not sure which lad is Trent, but God can tell.

Brent fell and got a bruise on his leg. If the twins will roll up the pant legs, then I can tell which twin is Brent.

The lads like to trick me, but the lads cannot trick God.

Fruit Juice

I like fruit juice. I will help Mom squeeze the fruit to make the juice. Since we do not like seeds in the juice, we will strain the pulp to get rid of the seeds.

We will put ice cubes in the juice to make it cold. Then Mom and I will sit on the porch and talk.

The Black and White Suit

He has a fine suit. His suit is black and white. His suit has stripes.

He likes fruit. He likes oats. He likes grass.

Can we tell his name?

Yes, we can tell. He is a ....

23

Here he is in his fine black and
white suit.

The Cruise

Tom's throat feels sore, and he is hoarse. Tom's mom and dad think it is best for Tom not to go on the cruise.

Tom is quite sad, but he will not moan or groan. He will not sass Mom and Dad. He will rest in bed. He will drink lots of fruit juice.

Tom plans to go with his chums on the next cruise.

A Long, Hot Trip

The sheik will take a long, hot ride. He must climb up high to sit. He will seize the rope, and the man will help him climb up.

The sheik has a cloth that keeps the sun off his face. He has on a long robe that he wraps close to him to keep the sand off his legs and feet.

The sheik plans to meet with some men at the palm trees. But it will be a long, hot trip for him.

27

What Weird Shapes!

What weird shapes! As the sun set, the tall trees on the shore made weird shapes on the lake. It was fun to watch the shapes change and move as the brisk wind came up.

The roar of the wind and the croaks from the frogs told us that it was time to go home. The weird shapes that we had seen were just a hoax.

My Toe! My Toe!

Joe goes to the game. He is sure his gang will win with his fine coach.

At the game Joe hurts his toe! He makes a sigh, "My toe! My toe! Woe is Joe! I will not be in the game. I must sit on the bench and soak my toe."

Joe yells for his gang to win as he sits on the bench. Joe yells till he is hoarse. He has a bad toe and a hoarse throat, but Joe is glad his gang won the game.

Zoe and Joe

Zoe will plant seeds. She will plant oats and beets.

Weeds are a foe to the small plants. Joe and Zoe will get rid of them.

Zoe hopes it will rain. The rain will make the small plants thrive. But the rain will make the weeds come up!

Then Joe and Zoe will have to hoe and hoe.

A Day for Mom

This is Mom's Day. This is not a day to play. We want to do some kind things for Mom. We will write her a note and place it on a tray. The note will say, "Thanks. We are glad we have such a nice mom. Love, May and Ray."

On the tray we will put Mom's brunch. We will take the tray to her. We hope Mom will like her tray and her brunch and her card.

Mom will say, "Thanks." Then she will give us both a big hug and a kiss. We hope this will make Mom's Day!

Play and Pray

We will romp and play with Dad. We will stay up and play till Mom says, "It is time for bed!"

Then we will all pray. I will pray first. Tim and Mom will pray. Dad will pray last.

Then we will kiss Mom and Dad. Mom will tuck me in my bed. Dad will tuck Tim in his bed.

Both Mom and Dad will hug and kiss Kay. Then Mom will put her in the crib and tuck her in.

A Fine Sheep Dog

Shep's job is to help Jed keep the sheep safe. When the sheep rest by the creek bank, Shep will not sleep. He will sit with Jed on a steep ledge and watch them.

Shep and Jed can rest a bit when all the sheep feed on the green grass.

At times a lamb will stray from the
flock. Shep will creep to that lamb. He
wants the lamb to come back. Shep
must not nip the white fleece of the
lamb. He will use his teeth to nip the
lamb's heels. Then the lamb will run to
get with the rest of the sheep.

At times a sheep might need to be freed from a thorn bush. Shep will bark. Jed will heed Shep's call. He will check to see what needs to be done. Jed might need to kneel by the sheep and free him. He might need to pull a thorn from the sheep's fleece or from his knee.

It is a big job to watch the sheep. Jed is glad that Shep is such a fine sheep dog.

A Dog of My Own

This big soft dog is my own. He is made from cloth. I made a nice bow for him.

My dog will not bark. He will not whine. He will not drink from a bowl. I know he has not grown an inch since he came to live with me. Still I love him just the same. It is such fun to show off my black and white dog.

What Is It?

There is a glow on Dad's face. He has a prize for us in the bag. I do not know what it is. Dad wants us to tell him if we can.

At first I am slow to think what might be in the bag. Rob thinks he knows. He asks Dad, "Will the prize grow?"

"No! No! No!" Dad told him.

I ask, "Is the prize one that we can throw?"

Dad tells me, "No! No! No!"

He smiles at us. Dad is slow to tell us what is in the bag, but he is sure both of us will like the prize.

43

Will Glue Fix It?

A rue plant was in the blue dish. The dish sat on Dad's desk.

When Sue comes in, she is sad to find that the dish is not on the desk. "Where can it be? I must find the rue plant and dish."

Sue has a clue. She spots some dirt on the desk, and she spots some dirt on the rug. Is her clue true?

As Sue walks to the desk, she finds the truth. The wind made the dish fall.

She hopes Dad can mend the dish with glue, but she is not sure the glue will work.

The Train Is Due

The train is due at nine. Dad is on the train. Since he has been on a trip, we have not seen him for a week.

We will be at the track as Dad's train rolls in. We will tell him that we are glad to see him.

When Mom sees Dad, she will give us the cue. Then we will start to sing. We have made up a fine song. The song will tell Dad that we love him.

Teach the Word

What a fine class Dick has to teach! The lads sit quite still while Dick speaks. He makes Christ's love clear and real to each lad. He speaks with ease as he tells the lads of God's Son, who gave His life on the cross.

At times Dick asks each lad to read a verse in class. Each lad speaks right up so that all can hear.

The lads will be in Dick's class all year. It will be a fine year for them. What a fine class!

Ten Men

Ten men were sick. Each man was so sick that he had to leave his home. The men came to ask the Lord to heal them.

The Lord was kind to the ten men. He made each of the men well. Each man was clean. He ran for his home. The ten men were so glad to be well.

One of the men who left came back to speak to the Lord. He fell at the Lord's feet to thank Him. The Lord had been so kind to heal this sick man.
The man was full of praise and love for the Lord.

What of the rest? Were there not ten sick men? Where were the nine? Just one man had come back to give thanks.

The Green Teal

One day Dad and I went to the pond to fish. As we sat on the bank, a strange duck came near.

This gray duck had green wings. He was quite small in size. He swam and swam on the pond. Since he kept his tail up as he swam, his tail did not get wet at all.

To get his lunch, the green teal made a quick dive in the pond. In no time at all, he held a fine fish in his nib. One gulp and it was gone.

Then the teal went for a short time to his home in the marsh close to the pond. He may have had a nest in the marsh.

Most of the day the strange duck swam on the pond. He was fun to watch. Dad told me that God has made blue teals that are much like green teals. Blue teals are not quite so small as the green teal on this pond.

Just as we got up to leave for home,
the green teal came straight up off the
pond. He did not fly at a slant but came
straight up. What a sight! He was
quick and full of grace.

Pick a Peach

Jay will climb
up high. He will
pick lots of fruit
from the tree. It
will take Jay
most of the day.
He will not quit
till all the fruit is
off the tree.

Dad and Jay will sit on the grass and
sort the fruit. Dad will talk with Jay as
he checks each peach for bad or soft
spots. Dad will quote a verse from
God's Word—"For the tree is known by
his fruit."

Dad tells Jay that his life is like a tree. Those who see Jay will know what kind of lad Jay is by what he speaks and by the way he acts.

Dad says Jay must speak kind words and do what is right. This will please Dad. Jay's life will please God. Jay will be glad. Those who watch Jay will know that he loves God.

The True Seal

The seal is fat and has lots of fur. This fits him for life in the sea. He slides in the sea with real ease.

Since he has a warm fur coat, he can be in the sea for a long time. His skin keeps him warm, and he will not get cold.

The seal swims fast for a short time. He loves to swim on his back.

God had a plan and a place for each kind of seal that He made.

Here is a true seal with her pup.

God gave the true seal holes for ears. The true seal may live all her life in the sea. She may not come to shore at all. Her calves or pups may be born in the sea. A pup can swim when he is born.

The true seal will blow and snort. She may make low groans with her throat, but she will not bleat or cry.

A Snow Fort

Joe was born in the North. He likes cold days and nights. He likes for the north wind to blow.

"A storm will bring snow," Joe said. "Then Tim and I can make a snow fort."

One day a strong wind came. Snow fell for a whole day.

The next day Joe said, "Where are the trees and the grass? I do not see them."

"The yard and the porch are white," said Tim. "This is a real storm. When the snow stops and the sun shines, we can make a snow fort in the back yard."

Joe and Tim wore coats and caps and gloves to keep them warm.

"We will put a torch at each end of
the fort," said Tim. "Dad will like that,"
said Joe. "He will blow the car horn to
let us know he is at home. We will
throw snow at him from the fort. He
will run to the porch so that we will not
hit him!"

"Then Mom will say that it is time to
eat,"said Joe. "And that will be grand!"

Black Crow

The black crow wants some lunch. He knows where the ripe corn grows.

The black crow spots a strange man. The man stands in the rows of corn. He has on an old, torn coat and a huge hat. The crow lands on the arm of this strange, weird man.

As the wind blows, the man's arm starts to bend low. The sleeve of the man's coat sways in the breeze.

The black crow must go. He will not
stay close to the strange man. He will
not get his lunch from the corn rows.

The strange man has kept the corn
rows safe. The crow will leave. He will
not come back while the strange man is
in the corn rows.

Four on the Fourth

Tim will be four on the fourth of June. And though it is not June yet, Jake has a gift for Tim.

The gift is soft, and Tim will love it, of course. He will not mourn when Jake gives him the gift. He will smile and be glad when he gets it.

What is the gift Jake gave to Tim?

Gourds

We will plant a row of gourds next to the fence. Of course, we hope the gourds will grow well so that we can use them this fall.

When the gourds are grown, we will pick them. Then we will wash and shine them. Mom will place four of the gourds on the ledge with some ears of maize.

If lots of gourds grow, I will take some to class. Miss Lee will let me show them to the class. Then she will place them on the fourth shelf.

God did not plan for us to eat gourds, but we like to gaze on them at home and in class.

Knead the Dough

Mom will mix a big batch of dough. She will use yeast to make the dough rise till it is high.

Sue wants to help Mom. Mom says Sue can knead the dough for her. Mom will show Sue what to do to knead the dough.

Mom will press, squeeze, punch, and then pat the dough. She will do it lots and lots of times. It is hard work to knead the dough.

Sue will knead the dough while Mom gets the pans. Mom will grease the pans and put some dough in each pan. The dough will rise in the pans. Then it will be time to bake each loaf. What nice loaves these will be!

Did He Spy the Pie?

Pete had lunch at twelve. At one he wants a snack! Can he find Mom's pie? He will check to see where Mom put the pie. Is it on the shelf? Is it in the stove? Where else can it be?

Did Pete find some pie? No, but he spied a can of pop and some fried ham on a bun. For his snack Pete will drink a can of pop and will munch on his ham.

A Home on the Wall

Her home was on the wall next to the gate.

Some spies came to her home. She let them in. She was nice and kind to the spies, but she had real fear that the spies might be hurt.

She had a plan. A large heap of flax might hide the spies from the mean men. She led the spies up the steps to the top of her home.

She had the spies lie flat. Then she hid them with dried stalks of flax.

When the mean men came with spears to find the spies, the spies were quite still. The mean men just made a quick glance at the flax but did not see the spies. Then the mean men left.

She crept back up to the spies. She made a plea for her life and the lives of her kin. The spies were glad to hear her. She had been kind to them. The spies might have died if she had not kept them safe.

The spies tied a red cord and let it fall from the wall to the dirt. Then the spies slid on the cord from the top of the wall to the dirt. The spies were safe.

The spies fled but left the red cord there on the wall. The spies did come back. She and her kin were kept safe.

Key to the Old Trunk

Mike has a key ring with lots of old keys on it. He must find the right key so that he and Sue can take a peek in the old, old trunk.

Mike tries three of the keys. At last he finds the right key. As he lifts the lid, it makes a squeak and a groan.

What fun to peek in this old, old trunk! These things in the trunk make Sue think of days long past. She likes the big hat with the wide brim. She thinks the three strands of beads are a real prize.

Mike finds a tall, black hat. He likes the old hat. Mike finds a cane to use when he walks. He tries on the long, gray cloak. The cloak has plush fur at the neck, and Mike feels grand when he puts on the cloak.

Mike will take the old clock from the trunk. He hopes that the clock will keep the right time.

Sue and Mike will put all the old clothes back in the trunk. Mike and Sue are glad that Mom let them take a peek. Mike will hang the key ring in a safe place so that the keys will not be lost.

Flies, Flies, Flies

There are flies on my pie;
There are flies on the chair;
There are flies on the tie—
And—there's a fly in my hair!
Such a pest is each fly,
To swat him, I'll try;
If this will not work,
My job I'll not shirk;
To get him—I'll do
or die!

Gauge the Tire

The tire on the truck seems to be low, but Dad cannot tell for sure. I will run to Pete's shop for Dad. Pete will lend me a tire gauge. I will take the gauge back to Dad.

He will use the gauge to judge if the tire is low. If it is, then Dad will add as much air as the tire needs. The tire gauge will be a big help to Dad. It will save him lots of time.

A Free Ride!

Ted sees a big flight of stairs. He thinks it will be more fun to slide on the rail than to walk on the steps.

When Ted gets to the end of the rail, he will walk up the flight of stairs and get back on the rail. What fun he will have!

This is a fast way to get from the top of the stairs. But it takes a while to walk back up to the top each time!

See the Glow

The rays of the sun are gone. In a short time it will be dark. The meal is done, and the last dish is on the shelf. We will all go sit on the front porch.

Ben and I will sit in the porch swing. We will sing and hum some old tunes. The night is warm and calm.

The porch light gives off a dim glow as Mom and Dad sit on a bench close by. The dim light makes a glow on Mom's face.

The old lamp shines on the desk by the drapes. It casts a soft glow on the yard. We spy lots of bugs that seem to be on fire.

The lights from the bugs flash off and on as the bugs fly here and there in the yard.

If we coax Dad, he may tell us an old, old tale. Dad has such a grand way when he tells these tales.

The warm air, the soft glow from the lights, and Dad's grand tale will make me think of sleep. When I start to doze, Dad will lift me in his arms and take me to my bed. The soft glow from my lamp will make me feel safe. Then I will sleep till morn.

Just Like a Queen!

Dad will give Mom a bunch of rose buds to pin on her best dress. He will put on his best suit. He will help Mom with her coat. Mom and Dad make quite a pair.

Dad will park the car near the curb at six. Then he will help Mom as she gets in the car. He will drive her to a nice place to eat. Dad treats Mom like a queen.

Dad will hold the chair for Mom. Mom and Dad will eat a fine meal.

As Mom and Dad eat, Mom will talk of the past. She thinks back to the first time she met Dad at church. She and Dad talk of that day. It has been twelve years since Mom and Dad first met.

Dad will give Mom a box. In the small box is a pearl broach. This is a fine day for Mom. Dad treats her just like a queen. What day is this?

The Peal
of the Bell

Sam is not weak.
He must be quite
strong to do his work
well.

With ease Sam pulls the big rope on the bell at the church. As he pulls the rope, he hears the long, clear peal of the bell. The tone hurts Sam's ears. The long toll of the bell can be heard for a mile from the church.

What can this peal of the bell mean? All in the small burg must come with haste. Some wake from sleep. Some run from play. Some rush from work. All meet at the church to hear the worst or to learn the best.

At times the man who leads this burg may tell of a fire or a storm. The creek may be full to the brim. Then he will need the aid of all who come.

But on this hot day the peal of the bell means more. It means the war is won! It means this land is free! The air is full of cries and praise to God. Some weep. Some pray. All are glad this day has come at last.

Whose Fault?

Mom wants to know what is the cause of such a mess. Whose fault is it?

The girls have been taught to tell the truth. Each girl knows who is to blame. Will the girls tell Mom who broke the lamp?

Will the girls tell the truth? I hope so. God's Word tells us that it is right to tell the truth all the time.

Pause for a Treat

I will pause from my work for a thick, rich treat. First, I will fill my dish with lots of ice cream. Then I will get the dark sauce. I will pour lots of this thick sauce on top of the ice cream.

This treat will make my day!

From Dawn Till Dark

The squaw has a dress made of skins. Long, black braids hang to her waist. On her neck are beads she has made of stones and shells.

The squaw sits on a rug and weaves with straw. She weaves from dawn till dark. At lunch time the squaw will stop her work to fix a meal for the brave and her son. The squaw works hard to care for those whom she loves.

Yawn at Dawn

It is dawn, and I just woke from a fine night of sleep. God kept me safe as I slept all night. I will yawn and stretch. Then I will ask God to help me do right and be kind all day.

I will thank God for this bright, fresh day. Then I will spend time in God's Word. This will help me start my day off right!

Crawl and Bawl

Peg saw this wee lad crawl to the edge of the porch. He had seen the pup in the yard. Peg did not want him to fall off the porch. If he fell, he might hit his jaw.

Peg ran to pick up the lad when she heard him bawl and bawl. Peg held the lad close.

The pup ran up the steps to play with the lad.

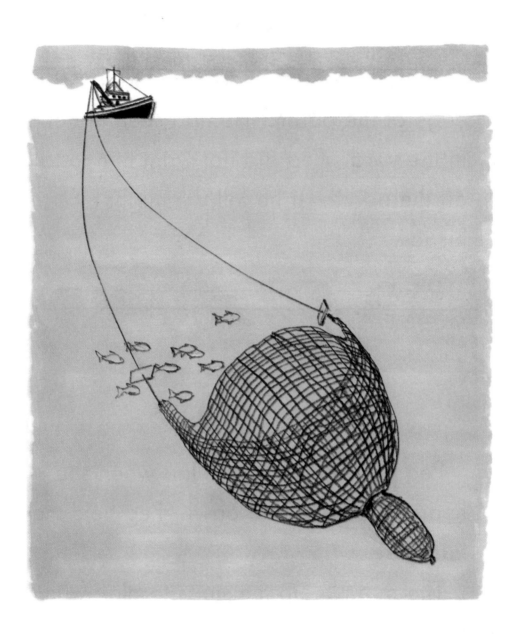

A Boat and a Trawl

The boat will drag the trawl. The trawl is a large net. As the boat moves, the trawl will fill with fish. Then the men will pull the trawl to the side of the ship. A man will crawl to the edge of the main deck. He will pull the trawl up on the deck.

The rest of the men will take all the catch of fish from the trawl. The raw fish will be sold to a fish shop near the shore.

Time to Sleep

The doe made a bed for her wee fawn. The fawn likes to sprawl on the nice bed of leaves and grass. He likes to sleep close to the doe.

The doe will stay with her fawn while he sleeps. She will watch so that no harm comes to her babe.

The fawn will sleep till dawn.

A Thorn in a Paw

Dawn's dad makes sure the laws of this land are kept. He works hard. Dad has a dog that goes with him when he works. Pal is a smart watch dog. He is a big help to Dawn's dad.

One day Dad came home with Pal. Dawn was glad to see Pal. She went to romp and play with Pal on the lawn.

Pal got close to the rose bush. A thorn got caught in Pal's paw. The thorn made Pal limp. It hurt him.

Dawn felt sad. She tried to pull the thorn from Pal's paw. It was quite deep. She ran to call Dad.

Dad came and got the thorn from Pal's paw. Dawn was glad. Pal was glad.

The Quilt

Faith has a large quilt. The quilt is made of bright scraps of cloth. No patch in the quilt is the same.

Faith will spread the quilt on her bed. She will not play or sprawl on her nice bed.

When it is time for bed, Faith will fold the quilt and lay it on a chair. Her mom has taught Faith to be neat and to make her bed each day.

Just the Right Time

See the snow! Lots of snow fell last night. The snow is deep. It is just the right time for a sleigh ride.

We will hitch the horse to the sleigh, and off we will go. The horse will neigh as he pulls the sleigh.

It is so cold that I can see my breath in the air. We have so much fun that I do not mind the cold.

At dusk we will turn the sleigh back and head for home. We will sing as we ride and breathe the crisp, fresh air.

The Bright Red Taw

It is lunch time. The lads will eat as fast as they can. They want to save most of their time to play a game. Each of the lads has a small sack tied to his belt.

When lunch is past, Frank and Bill will run to the yard. Frank will use a sharp stick to draw a large ring in the dirt. When the ring is drawn, the lads will take their sacks from their belts. They will dump the sacks at the edge of the ring.

Each will kneel next to the ring. Bill will pick up his bright red taw. It is made of clear glass, and it shines in the sun. Bill will aim his taw with care. What is the name of the game the lads like to play?

Paul Helps Dad

Paul wants to help his dad with the farm work. Paul's mom thinks they need to rake the back yard first. Paul knows that they will need a rake, a hoe, and a spade to do what his mom wants them to do.

Paul is glad that his dad made such a nice cart. It will be fun to haul things in his big cart.

First, Paul and his dad will rake the dead grass from the lawn. What a big job! They will pile the grass in a big heap. Then they must load it in the cart and haul it to the dump.

Next Dad and Paul will spade a small place by the fence. Mom must have a hedge and some shrubs there. They will use the spade, the hoe, and the rake.

Paul is glad that his dad taught him to work hard and not to quit till the job was done!

What Fun!

First, they will stuff his plaid shirt with straw. They will stuff him so full that the man will be quite plump.

Next Gale will paint a broad smile on the man's face. She will use bright red paint. Phil will laugh at the man's face.

Then Phil will place an old, old hat on the man's head. Phil got the old hat from the junk man.

The straw man is quite a sight as they tie him up on the big stick. Since he does not weigh much, he will bend and sway in the wind.

Phil and Gale will haul the straw man to the corn patch. When the crows see the straw man flap his arms from left to right, they will caw and caw. Then they will fly from the corn.

What fun to watch the straw man scare the crows!

The Gift

Grace will wrap the gift. The gift is great in size. She must not break the string as she wraps the gift.

Then Grace will move the gift from the ledge. She will set it on the chair. The gift will break if it falls from the chair. Can we tell what the gift is?

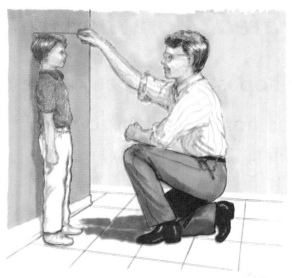

What Is My Height?

I will stand up tall next to the wall. I will stand quite still. Dad will check to see if I have grown since last month. Then Dad will write my height and the date on my chart.

Next month Dad will check to see if I have grown more. It is fun to keep track of my height each month.

Steaks on the Grill

Pete hopes this will be a fine day. He does not want it to rain. Dad and Pete will grill steaks. Mom wants her steak done well. Dad and Pete want rare steaks.

Pete will place the coals on the grill. Then he will stand back as Dad lights the grill. Dad will place six steaks on the grill.

Dad and Pete will play ball till the steaks are done. When the steaks are done, Mom will bring a huge plate to the grill and let Dad pile the steaks on the plate.

A Great Feud

There may be a great feud at dawn. The cause of the feud will be the bread crumbs that I have thrown on the lawn for the birds.

Lots of birds will fly to the lawn to eat the crumbs. A large, black crow will dive from the air. He will peck at the birds. He will flap his wings till he can push his way to the bread crumbs.

The black crow is full of greed. He
wants to snatch all of the bread crumbs.
He does not want to share with the rest
of the birds. The feud starts. Who
will win?

We laugh when birds feud, but it does
not please God when we feud.

New Shoes—Old Shoes?

Are those shoes new? No, the kind old man does his work on old shoes. He can make Dale's old shoes seem just like new.

He may nail a pair of soles on the shoes. He may need to mend a rip or put new heels on the shoes.

Dale likes to watch him make the old shoes as nice as new.

Few in a Pew

We came to church. We knew we were not late. We did not pause to talk but came right in and sat in a pew. Dad, Mom, and I did not fill the whole pew. We sang lots of hymns. I sat quite still and did not squirm as the man of God taught from God's Word.

Some folks came in late. Just one pew was left at the back of the church. They all had to sit in that back pew. Whew! It was a full pew!

We were glad that we were on time. There were just a few in my pew. We had lots of space and did not need to squeeze so close.

Learn a truth from me: those who come late have to take a back pew.

Folks who want the best pew need to come to church on time. Then they can sit close to the front, and there will be just a few in each pew.

Let It Brew

Walt wants to brew a pot of tea. He will place the pot on the stove and turn the knob to "high."

As Walt waits, he fills a glass jar with new screws. Walt did not watch as he set the jar next to the stove. Since it was near the edge, it fell off.

Whew! The glass jar did not break, but most of the screws flew from the jar. Just a few screws were left in it.

When all the screws are back in the jar, Walt will fill his cup from the pot. Then he will add a tea bag and let it brew till it is just right for him. The tea will not need to brew long since Walt does not like strong tea.

A Chief and a Brave

The chief and his brave will go to the east field. Each has his bow at his side. The chief will teach his son just what to do.

The chief and the brave will sneak up close to the deer. The chief aims his

bow. Will he pierce the deer? He thinks so! But—no! The deer flees. The deer is safe!

The chief and brave walk on. They hear a hawk squawk as it dives to catch its prey.

The chief and the brave make a jaunt to the stream. They cast a net in the stream and catch lots of fish. They will take the fish home to the squaw. She will make a fine feast from the fish.

At the Pier

The ship is in dry dock by the pier for just a brief time. The crew will work hard to get the ship in great shape for the sea. A few of the crew will paint the hull of the ship. A few will check all the thick, huge ropes. One of the crew will screw all the bolts that are not tight. The ship will be in shape for the sea in no time at all since the crew will do such a fine job.

Off They Flew!

The crows flew to the field to eat grain. The man made of straw did not scare the crows. Shane saw the crows and ran to the field. He had to climb the fence.

The crows saw Shane, but they did not leave. They did not seem to fear him.

Shane thought, "I will scare them if I yell." But no, the crows did not fly from the field.

"I will scare them if I wave my arms," he thought. But still they did not move.

At last Shane had a plan. He knelt in the grain and chose a large stone. He threw the stone with all his might. The stone did not hit the crows, but it did make them squawk. Off they all flew!

Who Did It?

What a crime! Who stole the loaf?
Who did it? Where is he?

We do not know. The sleuth has a
plan to catch the thief. He has a strong
glass. He will check the prints to see
who made them. Who do you think did
it? Do you know?

The thief was a bird! He stole the
fresh bread and left just crumbs.
A jay did it! Oh, what a crime!

Eyes in the Dark

Dad and Jean will walk on the path. At night the path is dark, but Dad has a light in his hand. The light will guide them as they walk through the dark night. Jean has no fear since Dad has a light.

Do you see a pair of eyes in the tree? Who do you think is there? Can it be a hawk? Is it a fierce wolf? Or might those eyes be the eyes of a cat? Jean and Dad are not sure, but they will not stop to find who is there.

Dad thinks the eyes are those of a wise bird who sleeps in the day but stays up at night. The bird's eyes are quite large, and he sees well in the dark. Name the wise bird.

Guess Which Hand

Greg has a gift for his sis. He wants her to guess which hand holds her gift. She thinks it is in his left hand, but it may be in his right hand.

She does not know. She must guess. Then Greg will give her the gift.

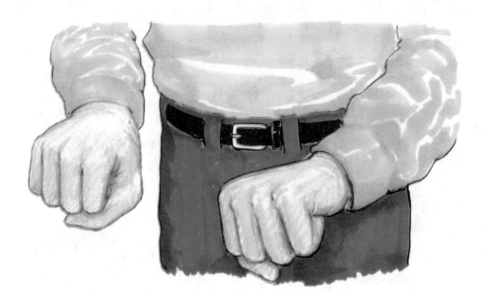

Build with Blocks

Mom bought the small tot some
blocks. He will build with these blocks.
What will he build? Can you guess?

Will he build a bridge or a church or a snow fort? Will he build a farm or a barn or a burg?

No, the young tot cannot build such hard things with his blocks. He will just try to stack his blocks up tall and straight.

The tot must touch each block with care. He cannot be rough. The blocks are light and do not weigh much.

The tot laughs as he plays with his blocks. Mom bought this fine gift for him. He will sit and play with the blocks for a long, long time.

They Made This Land Great

They came on a small ship. They came
to this land to be free. The trip was long
and hard. Some got sick on the trip.

Each day they would read God's Word
and each would pray. This was a real

help to them on the long trip. They had
great faith that God would bring them to
this new land.

The first year in this land was rough for
all of them. A lot of them were sick. Half
of them died. But when fall came, none
of them left this land to go back on the
ship to their old land. They felt they must
stay here in this new land where they
would be free. They could build their
own homes and have their own church.
They would not quit. They would not
give up. They would not leave. They
made this land great. Who were they?

As a lad, he told the truth. He said he could not tell a lie. He had a real love for God, his kin, his horse, and his land. This lad did fine work at home and in class. He wrote with great care. He was neat as he wrote lots of rules that he would use as a guide in his life.

Since he had such a great love for God, he would pray for God to guide him. He led men in a war as they fought to keep this land free.

He was the first man we chose to lead this young land. All had a deep love for this fine man. He made this land great. Who was he?

This tall lad could not go to class much. But he had a will to learn. His mom taught him to read at home. He would stretch in front of the fire at night and read for a long time. He read God's Word. Since he read God's

Word so much, he knew most of what he had read.

When he grew up, he went to class to learn law. He was kind and did what he could to help those in this land who were in need.

We chose him to lead this great land. This was a hard time. We were at war. But this man had a hope that all could be free. He led this land well. He had

a great love for God. He died when a mean man shot him. This tall man made this land great. Who was he?

We must love this land and keep its laws. When we are grown, the Lord may use some of us to help keep this land great.

Pray for this land each day. Ask God to guide all those who lead this great land. Be sure to thank God each day for this land in which we live. This great land lets us be free to love God, to pray, and to do right. "Thanks, God, for this great land. Please keep it free."

Corn on the Hearth

Dad and John will pop a pan of corn. Dad will kneel on the brick hearth. John will kneel next to Dad.

The sparks from the fire make a soft glow. Dad will talk with John as the corn pops in the pan. Dad will quote a verse from God's Word. The verse is, "Lord, help me."

Dad tells John that this verse is a fine verse to learn and keep in his heart. The verse can help John when he takes a test in class. It is a verse that will help John when hard jobs need to be done. John will learn the verse. He will use it much in his life. The verse will be a big help to John.

The Sword and the Shield

This lad plans to fight a tall, tall man. He has a sword and a shield that King Saul gave him to use.

The shield is huge, and it weighs a lot. The lad does not want to use the king's shield nor his sword.

He knows the tall, tall man is fierce, but he knows God will keep him safe.

The lad will use five stones and his sling. He has no fear in his heart. He knows God will take care of him. Who is the lad?

145

Reach the Hook

The small girl shook the snow from her wool coat. Then she stood up on her toes to reach the hook made of wood. She hung her coat on the hook and went to her chair. It was time for class to start.

The Hike

Steve went for a hike in the woods. He thought it was great sport to jog on the path. He had a good time.

Steve did not look at the path in front of him. He did not see a sharp twig till his left foot struck it. Steve fell! His foot hurt!

Steve had to hop to a log. It felt good
to soak his sore foot in the brook.

At last Steve could walk. Next time
Steve will watch the path when he runs
or jogs in the woods!

Mom's Cook Nook

Dad took three hooks from a bag. He went to Mom's cook nook. With a short tap, tap on the wall, Dad put the three hooks in just the right place. Mom hung a mug on each hook.

Next Dad hung a shelf on the wall in the nook. The shelf was for Mom's books. A good cook needs lots of books!

Dad and Mom stood back and took a good look at the nice nook. Mom thought Dad had done a good job. Mom gave Dad a hug and a big "thank you."

The Best Book of All

James loves to
read this good
Book. It is the
best Book of all.
It is God's Word.

This Book gives
James much help. This Book tells him of
God's love. All of this Book is true.

James must read this good Book each
day. This Book gives him good news
from the Lord. James is glad to have his
own Book to read.

Can you tell the name of this good
Book?

Nine Ducks in the Rain

Nine ducks stood in the rain. Each duck went splash, splash. It was fun to wade and splash. It was fun to walk in the rain with short steps and to sway from side to side.

The first duck stood next to a tree at the edge of the woods. He shook the drops of rain from his back. He took a quick look at the eight ducks. Each duck shook the drops of rain off his back and came to him. Nine ducks stood in the woods!

The Coal Bin

Brent and Gail went to play in the coal bin. What a place to play!

Brent got soot on his face and hands and arms. Soot was on his shirt and pants and shoes.

Gail got soot on her wool skirt. She got soot on her face and legs. Soot was on her sleeves and her shoes. "Mom will not like the way we look," said Gail. "What will we do?"

Brent tried to get rid of the soot. He shook his feet and legs. He tried to dust his shirt and pants. The soot still clung to him and his clothes.

154

Gail tried to brush the soot off, but it would not budge!

Next time Gail and Brent will find the right place to play.

A Friend in Need

A harsh wind blew. The air was cold. Jed shook. He did not have on a wool coat. His light coat did not break the wind. His hands were cold. He had no warm gloves.

As Jed thought of his need, Miss Stone saw him and knew that Jed was in need of help. She gave him a wool coat and red gloves. She took Jed home in her car.

Jed's kind friend told him and his mom of the Lord. The next day she came and took them to church with her. She was a friend in their time of need.

My Pet Goose

Look at my pet goose. He is white. My goose likes to run loose in my yard. My goose snoops in the box.

Next he snoops in the boots. Then he snoops at the rose in bloom. At noon my pet goose eats his food from the pan. My pet goose likes to snoop at lots of things.

The Chores

Mom has some chores for Ann and Jane. She will let each girl choose her own chore.

Ann will choose to take the broom and sweep the room. Jane will choose to fix the food for lunch at noon.

Both girls will do the chores well. This will please Mom. It will please God, too.

A Bad Mood

Pete is not in a nice mood. He just sits on the stool and broods.

Why is Pete in such a bad mood? Pete did not get his way. He could not go to the pool with his pals. His pals went to the pool to swim. Pete was sick with a cold and had to stay at home.

Poor Pete! He needs to smile. He needs to get off the stool and end his bad mood. He needs to go play or go help Dad.

Did Pete's bad mood please God?

The Moon

God made the moon. The moon shines at night and lights up the sky. I am glad God made the moon. I am glad it shines at night as I sleep in my soft bed. Thank you, God, for the bright moon so high up in the sky.

I like these lines that tell of the moon —

> I see the moon,
> The moon sees me;
> God bless the moon,
> And God bless me.

163

Big Cat

Shawn went to the zoo. He saw a big cat with large paws and sharp claws. This cat had black stripes.

Shawn saw the big cat eat raw meat. The big cat held the meat in his paws while he tore it with his sharp claws. The food was gone in no time at all.

Can you guess the name of this big cat?

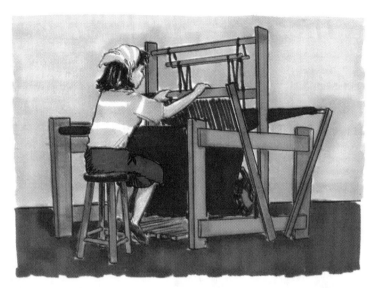

Beth and the Loom

Beth will weave a rug on a loom. She will sit on a stool in front of the loom. Beth will loop the yarn on the loom. She will make sure the yarn is smooth on the loom as she weaves the rug. Beth will weave on the loom till noon. The rug will be huge when it is done. Beth will do a nice job on her rug.

These are my Friends

This friend takes great care of my teeth. He is my friend. Who is he?

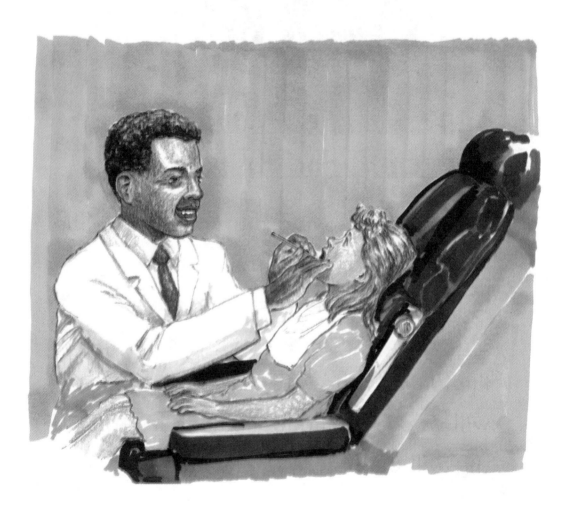

This kind friend works in a room full
of books. She helps me choose good
books from the shelves. She lets me
sit and read. Who is she?

Day or night, this friend will come if we need him. We have no fear since we know this friend will bring his crew to stop the fires. Who is he?

This friend is quick to come if I am
lost or need help. He keeps an eye on
those who might break the laws of my
land. I trust this friend. He works hard
to keep me safe. Who is he?

In church this friend will preach God's Word to me.

He will show me from God's Word that God loves me. He will tell me to let God's Word guide my life each day.

He is glad to pray with me when I ask him. This friend loves God and he loves me. I love this friend. Who is he?

Who is this friend? She taught me to write and to spell. This friend has taught me lots and lots of new things.

Best of all, she has taught me to read. She has taught me to love good books. I can read God's Word—the best Book of all!

When I feel good or when I feel bad, this friend cares. He takes the time to make sure that my health is the best. Who is he?

Here are my kin. They are the best
friends I have on earth. God gave me
just the right mom and dad to love
and care for me. He put me in just
the right home. These are my best
friends on earth. Who are they?

You have met some of my friends. Let me share with you the Best Friend of all. Do you know Him? He is God's Son. He died for my sins. He loves me all the time. I can talk to Him when I pray. I can learn of Him when I read His Word. He knows me well. He sees all I do. He hears all I say. He is the Best Friend of all! Is He your Best Friend?